The Wanderer

—— A POET'S JOURNEY ——

Selected Poems

by

Robert Emmons

CAPRA PRESS
MEMORABLE BOOKS SINCE 1969
SANTA BARBARA

A Robert Bason Book
Published by Capra Press
155 Canon View Drive
Santa Barbara, CA 93108
www.caprapress.com

Jacket and book design by Frank Goad, Santa Barbara

Library of Congress Cataloging-in-Publication Data

Emmons, Robert, 1934-
The wanderer / Robert Emmons ; foreword by Chryss Yost.
p. cm.
"A Robert Bason Book"—T.p. verso.
ISBN 1-59266-048-7
I. Title.

PS3555.M5229W36 2005
811'.54—dc22
2004013455

Edition: 10 9 8 7 6 5 4 3 2 1
First Edition

To my wife Christine

a constant source
of loving inspiration

ACKNOWLEDGMENTS

This book would not have been possible without the unflagging support of my wife Christine. I must also thank my personal assistant Karen Treviño whose editorial efforts and creative suggestions were invaluable. Special thanks also to Chryss Yost for the kind words and thoughtful introduction and to Bob Bason and Rich Barre of Capra Press for their enthusiastic support of this project.

FOREWORD

Poetry is a way of seeing. The poet looks beyond the surface of things, carefully observing the interior tensions and longings that are undetected by the eye. In this way, words are merely a lens through which one experiences poetic vision. With this book in your hands, you hold the lens through which Robert Emmons views the world.

Imagine, for example, a sailboat battered by a sudden tempest. A filmmaker would capture this drama by showing the waves pounding against the deck, the crew huddled in the cabin, the boat tossed like a small cork in the churning sea. The next scene might show the resilient captain steering into a calm harbor after the storm has passed. The filmmaker can document exactly how the storm looks, full of black water and foam, and how the morning sunlight sparkles off the water once the storm subsides.

What film cannot capture is the way in which this small, sudden storm has changed the ship's captain by giving him a renewed appreciation for the details of each day.

Robert Emmons brings the perspective of a sailor who has survived his storms to witness many glorious sunrises. His poems are invitations to experience the world and be changed by it. He understands that epiphanies are rarely announced with a bolt of lightning and studies the small but significant occurrences that develop our humanity. "I mark the scene," he writes in "Singing in the Rain." In marking the scene, he asks readers to share what he finds in the moment: an opportunity to witness love, devotion, ambition, or, too often, regret.

Considering his extensive experiences and travels, it is hardly surprising that Emmons' sixth book covers a wide range of subjects. The three sections of his book – "The Earth," "The Sea," and "The Sky" – appropriately suggest that nothing is out of the poet's reach. Emmons' passion for life is the basis for all his poems, whether celebrating life's pleasures or mourning lives squandered and lost.

The Wanderer includes a varied cast: fishermen, ice cream vendors, terrorists, and others. In "A Very Driven Man" and "A Manufactured Man," Emmons uses his sensibilities as an art collector to create a precise portrait of visible success masking personal failure. His own experiences as an entrepreneur and executive enhance his description of the bitter, lost souls:

> created by an
> image of desire.
> but ephemeral and transitory,
> betrayed by a shallow
> desperate inner being.

(from "A Manufactured Man")

Emmons' compassion takes him from the boardroom to the battlefield. For thousands of years, poets have described the sorrows and loss of war, giving voice to those fallen in battle. Emmons summons the specters of war in a young fighter in Iraq ("Fallouja") and in the tear-stained obituary for a Union soldier ("The Attic"). The tragedy of war is felt one soldier at a time, each life precious:

> Teardrops still stained the clipping
> from the Boston Globe. One hundred
> years and more could not
> contain a mother's grief as she
> passed eternity in sorrow.
>
> (from "The Attic")

If sorrow is present in these poems, it is because Emmons deeply cherishes life. Most of his poems radiate an appreciation for life's bounty. Passion, beauty, and joy triumph. Through his eyes, even the waning day becomes a ritual of desire:

> Through it all, the pale moon
> hides in the silver sky. An
> alabaster presence, lurking,
> waiting for the sun to douse
> its daily fire and allow the
> moon to capture the earth in
> a lover's sweet embrace.
>
> (from "Earth")

He embraces the world as lover, father, traveler, and poet. With these many roles to choose from, he seems most himself in love poems, such as "A Warm Blanket" and "Lunar Eclipse," and in poems such as "Isla Espirito Santo" and "Tuscan

Morning," which evoke simple days, relaxing in a newly discovered landscape:

> The hillside vineyards
> reached out for the
> day's warm caress
> as the bells of San Gregorio
> peeled out in
> joyous rapture.
> Once again God
> had given his blessing
> to his chosen ones.

(from "Tuscan Morning")

Perhaps the words that best fit these poems are found in a line from "Skies." In this homage to cloud-gazing, the poet declares:

> But most of all, my favorites
> are the Cumulus with their
> silver towers reaching far up
> into the heavens. They call to
> me to scale their heights with
> a promise of eternal life
> if I would only try.

Like clouds, these poems, too, are an invitation to visit new heights.

—CHRYSS YOST, Co-Editor of *California Poetry*, Santa Barbara

CONTENTS

The Earth…

Earth

The earth spins frantically
trying to keep pace with
the sun, that ancient
fireball in the sky. The
sun sits motionless on its
lofty perch and dispenses
life, like a friendly
neighborhood pharmacist
with limited hours of service.
A careful potion measured
with great care dispensed
daily, the dosage dependent
on the hour and the season.

The earth responds with joy
at the sun's prescription of
life. It celebrates with an
endless bounty of color
and nourishment for its
earthlings. Sadly in winter
the sun loses its way, its
duty lost in gray, morose
cloudy days. A foreboding
harbinger of what could yet
someday be.

The earth celebrates the
sun god's importance but
resents its dependency, its
heavy burden, the all
consuming fear that the
sun will move away leaving
but another lifeless asteroid
floating in the universe.

Through it all, the pale moon
hides in the silver sky. An
alabaster presence, lurking,
waiting for the sun to douse
its daily fire and allow the
moon to capture the earth in
a lover's sweet embrace.

Cold Morning

The sun had not
arisen from
its place of rest
but the light
of the dawning quietly
tiptoed into my room.

Silvery fingers danced
across my face and
pried open my eyes
to an awakening
gray universe.

I shivered and
buried my head
beneath the soft
warm pillows
seeking a place
to hide from a
frigid threatening day.

The winter fog
held the moment captive
its tentacles clutching
at the hillside
in an ocean's
death grip.

Reluctantly, I
emerged from my
place of hiding
guiding my feet
across the arctic
floor to an unkind
waiting world.

A Manufactured Man

He was a picture
    of success.
The power wardrobe
    ever present,
never a blemish,
    every hair in place.
A cool detachment
    behind blue eyes
that could sparkle
    or burn your soul.
A smile that could stop
    traffic on Rodeo Drive.
A low commanding
    well schooled voice
that never exceeded
    its limits.
Women swooned when
    he entered a room.
They told stories to each other
    of what they might do
      were they to spend
        a night alone.

But beneath the veneer
of privilege and promise,
dwelt another man.
A man of failed relationships,
of marriages gone wrong,
of distant children,
and few true friends.
A façade carefully crafted
but lost in the
terrors of the night.
A manufactured man
created by an
image of desire.
but ephemeral and transitory,
betrayed by a shallow
desperate inner being.

Sold at Auction

The woman's eyes were cast down
as she lay nude upon the chaise,
the bowl of ripe fruit with
open pomegranate lips lay on the
table before her, enticing her lover.

I stood transfixed by the Lebasque
painting. Its beauty and sensuousness
were overwhelming.

A small middle-aged woman appeared
at my shoulder.

"My *grand-mère* was his lover
until he went away. The painting
has hung in my mother's house
and then mine for more than seventy
years. My *grand-père* was a very jealous man,
he would not allow it in his house."

"I am sorry to sell it, but we have
debts that must be paid.

Mais c'est la vie.

Hopefully the buyer will
give it great care."

The auction commenced and soon
Lot 64 was presented for bid.
My agent, who secretly sat across
the room from me, bid aggressively,
winning over a disappointed dealer
from London.

Afterward, the woman approached again.
"*Monsieur*, do you know who purchased
my *grand-mère*?"

I told her it was I, and that the
painting would have the best of care
and hang in a place of honor in my
home in Santa Barbara.

"Perhaps I might come and visit
my *grand-mère* someday?"

I assured her she would always
be welcome and bid *adieu*.

Alex Johnson

"You have only one life Bobby, be sure
to live it well." My mother's admonition,
somewhat surprising coming from a
Catholic's lips. I do believe she wished for
a heaven but the journey was the real
thing. She could have been a Jesuit.

Quite a contrast with my boyhood friend
Alex Johnson. An existentialist he was not.
The distant future dominated his life.
He lived penuriously for his retirement
from the time of his twenty-fifth birthday.
You had to twist his arm to spend a dollar
in his youth, and as success reluctantly
came his way, thrift became his god. His
bankbook became his altarpiece.

When Helen left him he was crushed. Not
to see her go, but despaired for what she
took with her. He would rail against
his partner of twenty-odd years to
whomever would listen. Her contribution
was never mentioned.

In her absence his miserly life became
more withdrawn, even more intense
as retirement loomed near. When the
chest pains came he was incredulous.
What a cruel joke! Life could not end
like this, he was not yet to the beginning!
The irony stuck deep in his throat as
he sucked his last breath.

The Black Hole

Last night was filled
with terror and disquiet
and yesterday seemed
never to end.

She had disappeared in the
afternoon leaving a note
on the kitchen table.
Everything had been packed
away in a place he could
never discover. She had
planned her escape for many
months and now she had
quietly stolen away.

She had been restless and
more secretive recently, but
after all these years, he
blamed it on the menopause.

She hated routine and life
had been too predictable.
Always the same faces,
the same places, the same
stories and too few glories.

Time was stealing her life
and she was frightened;
she longed for an adventure.
He was sameness to a fault.
He ignored her pleas. He
had settled in.

But now the day after, he
walked the silent house and
sobbed inside. She had left
him to die alone without
a consoling touch and he
had fallen into a black
hole from which he would
never climb.

A Very Driven Man

He was a seeker of greatness.
At least that was what he liked
to call himself.

Others used words such as
malcontent, opportunist, and
perfectionist, and some words
much less flattering.

He was always pushing
forward, never satisfied,
convinced that Elysian Fields
lie just beyond the next ridge.

He was not one to suffer fools.
If one could not keep pace, he
would leave them beside the
road and push onward. Nothing
could interfere with his quest.

While some admired his sense
of purpose, others shook their
heads in sadness.

A very driven man.

The stroke occurred on a Sunday
afternoon as he worked at his
desk in his office.

Suddenly, his world turned upside down.

He lost his speech and short term
memory, he was partially paralyzed.
He was forced to slow to a stop.

Those he had little time for were
now the caregivers who gave him
succor. His life became one of
tolerance, patience and most galling
to him, dependence.

The power player was no more!

He, in his fifty-eighth year, had become
a child. But mother and father were
no longer there to care for him. Gone
also were wives number one, two, and
three. The friends he had no time for
had also drifted away.

His world was now populated by his
distant doctor, his impatient male nurse,
and Mrs. Turner, his long suffering
housekeeper. Occasionally, one of his
children would write, but rarely.

Imprisoned in his silent, powerless
world he waited, but for what?

Remembrance of Things Past

Her beauty was not timeless,
the spa could do only so much.
A well-lived life and four
husbands had taken a toll.
The charm was still there, but
a shadow of melancholy now
rested on her shoulder. Even
her laughter was muted by
a gray curtain of unkept
promises. Her sensuality would
give off flashes of other times,
but they soon passed with the
chill of an evening summer
storm. On more than one
occasion, the remembrance
of things past would drop a
tear across her painted cheek.
Embarrassed, she would turn
her head and pass a quiet
moment. Then, forcing a wistful
smile across her blushing face,
she would offer a hollow excuse
and quickly flee to the comfort
of her silent empty home.

The Order of the British Empire

Some thought Reginald Taylor
    an exceptionally confident man
overbearing and at times obnoxious
    and quick to raise a hand

A man who seemingly had everything
    one could possibly want
and yet beneath the thin veneer
    a great need to boast and flaunt

He would go to his club and speak of
    much more than he had actually done
for an OBE was an obsessive quest
    for which he had doggedly run

But the Queen knew more than he
    thought she could possibly know
for she had learned of the secret gardens
    to which he had taken a hoe

And so she let it be known that
    honors would not come his way
and his life would never see
    the dawn of that special day.

When he heard the news a mask
    appeared on his oft too eager face
and he seemed to put aside
    his cudgel, sword and mace.

With nothing left to live for
    in his far too focused world
he shot himself in Surrey
    his flag of honor ne'er unfurled.

An African Afternoon

A lion roars a challenge
floating over a torrid
summer sky, but the dry
yellow hillside is silent in
response, its echo lost in
the heat of the day.

The antelope raises its head
and leaves its thirst to wait
aside the river bed, ever
anxious and always alert.

The warthog growls its
displeasure as it feeds
on yesterday's leftovers
unwilling to be interrupted
despite the risk.

The zebras break into a
panic and run away from
the reverberating challenge,
in their terror, escape
their only thought.

The bull elephant raises his
trunk and trumpets in
return as if to say,
"I rule here, who
dares to send a challenge?
I will not tolerate an interloper."

The Land Rover crashes through
the underbrush, its unnatural
presence scarring an
African afternoon.

The Source of Evil

The mind of the terrorist is
beyond my comprehension
the source of such evil
a great puzzlement.

What would turn a
sweet young innocent girl
into a school bus bomber
killing equally innocent
children?

What would turn a kindly
Moroccan tailor into a mass
murderer in Spain?

It truly cannot be Islam
for Mohammed was a
gentle Prophet of simple
ways, teaching the need
for learning, respect
and love.

Why in the name of
Mohammed have they
rejected his teaching,
put aside his Koran and
embarked on a journey
to a land of desperation,
destruction and consummate
evil?

Where will this madness
take us, to a world of
retribution for retribution,
evil upon evil, terror
for terror's sake?

How can we stop this
insanity and find the path
to a world of tolerance,
peace, brotherhood and love?

I have no answers only
heartsick questions heaped
upon heartsick questions.

Fallouja

He had been moving
    fast, for two days,
        forty-eight hours
           without sleep,
chasing phantoms across
    the bleak countryside.

The convoy had been hit hard,
    creating havoc, outside of
        Fallouja.

A land mine had destroyed
    their armored personnel carrier
        and with it Billy the Kid,
           the laughing one.

They had joined the National Guard
    to play soldier,
        one weekend a month
           part-time.

The call up surprised them,
    much excitement,
        they were going
           to kick ass.

But now Billy was gone,
    body parts in a bag, and
        he was left alone.

The Iraqi insurgents were
    playing hit and run,
        but they were closing in on
            them fast, chasing them
                nonstop.

They had to pay
    for Billy and Jack and Tommy.

He was the avenger,
    the angel of death,
        the twenty-year-old
            survivor.

The mixed-up kid
    with all the questions
        from the farm in Fresno;

Why was he here?
    How did this happen?

Why did they spit in his face
     for the freedom he offered?

Where would this all end?
     Was he the next to lie entombed,
          mummified in black plastic?

His anguished thoughts were blown
     away as the rocket tore into
          his careening truck.

He flew through the sulphurous air
     and tumbled into a roadside
          ditch

His bloody hands took a desperate.
     inventory; to joyfully discover
          he was still whole.

Tears fell down his face as he
     prayed to God to take him home.

Home, to his father's farm,
     and its peaceful fields
          of snow white cotton.

The Sparrow

The sparrow
    crashed
against my polished
    silver window pane
it spun and fluttered
    helplessly
        to the ground.
Lured by the vase
    of tired
        blue irises,
resting on
    my kitchen table,
it blundered on
    until the window
        claimed its victim,
its vibrating body
    giving up life
        by the second,
as nature showed
    no mercy.

The Innocents

The innocents always pay the price
no matter the geography, the story
almost never
                    changes

The power brokers joust in a
bloodless conflict, with rarely
a personal cost, safe in their
warm cocoons ordering others to
to make the ultimate
                    sacrifice

The children with limbs torn
asunder bathed in showers
of blood, know not the reason
                    why

Foot soldiers speak with great
bravado but shake with tremors
in the night chill, while pilots
rain terror in their electronic
onslaught, somehow morality is
lost in the obscurity of distance
but surely remembered in
                    tomorrow's nightmares

War is never the answer, millenniums
pass and generations of innocents
suffer meaninglessly but lessons
are rarely learned and never
                    remembered

Through the centuries the misdeeds of
the conqueror somehow vanish from the
minds of those who follow, only victories
remembered with their inhumane brutality,
                    forgotten in time

The initiators will never
cleanse the spots of blood from
their hands and no amount of
rhetorical scrubbing can remove
their sin while their blathering
justifications are lost in the
night sounds of the scarred
and suffering innocents
                    left behind

The Baja

A land of contrast and
paradox, a borderland
of drugs, violence and
despair, a religious people
that God seems to have
forsaken.

A lusty land of hard, dry
soil, farmers and gentle
fishermen, a land of
angry stone-faced Aztecs
and laughing mariachis.

A desert land, hot with
desire, its lurid heat
radiating from its hilltops
and finding its way to
its efflorescent seas.

A land that too often
sends its children to the
North with only a distant
hope of reclaiming them
in their old age.

A land of familial love and
devotion, a land of respect
and pride, a pioneer land
that thirsts for its future
of fairness and prosperity.

The Ashes of Remembrance

I sift the dusty
ashes of remembrance
grown cold with time
searching for you

knowing you were there
but now only ashes
blowing silently away
with an autumn breeze

white smoke drifting
on a Vatican morning
promising so much
but now almost lost
with naught but
a far distant receding
elusive memory

The Poet

He would awake in the
middle of the night
and try to stave off
the mind stream of words
that fought through the
brambles of his subconscious.

The ideas, phrases, word
thoughts, relationships
crowding out each other
in a rush to find their way to
paper. He tried desperately
to sleep but too often failed.

He would quietly slip out of
bed, careful not to awaken
his sleeping lover, and find
his way to paper and pen.
In the quiet of the night's
blackness a poem would be
born, wrenched from the
womb of his mind.

Finally, at peace, he would
turn again to sleep.

The Sea...

The Sea

The sea shimmered in
the late afternoon sun
while silver white clouds
danced across a distant
azure sky.

The seashells fell one upon
another in a desperate
attempt to flee the waves
that bore them to the shore,
then helplessly surrendered and
fell back.

The seabirds darted among
the salt foam and then
slipped away only to return
with the next cascading wave.
Again and again they joyously
performed the pas de deux
of nature's ballet.

The wooden skiff touched
the sand, then fell back
into the arms of the sea,
tugging on its anchor that
lay buried on the beach.

The rhythms of the
afternoon captivated me
as I sat in wonder
at nature's poetry.

The Tranquil Shore

I walk the tranquil shore
a quiet foreboding my ever
closer companion. I push
him aside and walk on alone.

The sea has been silenced,
but the storm should thrust
itself upon us with the
morning light.

A pebble lies in my path,
I choose to step around
it, not risking that I
might kick it aside
and spoil a magical moment.

A sandpiper rushes toward me
and then stops suddenly, as if to say,
"Who is this intruder?" I pause
and stand quietly until he
dances away.

A clam struggles to right itself
from its unnatural position in
the sand. I turn it over.

Up ahead, two lovers embrace
and capture a moment they
might have lost forever.

I press on as the sun slowly
slips beyond the far horizon
sadly closing a crimson curtain
on a perfect day.

The Crossing

The tossed sea gave way
    to a frenzy of gale winds
        and cascading waves

Their sloop was thrown
    across its roiling surface
        seemingly without direction or purpose

They huddled below and
    desperately fought the wheel
        to no avail

They thought of home and love
    and promises unkept
        and too many things undone

Was this the end
    two incomplete lives thrown up
        on the coast of Sardinia
            battered, broken, and unfinished?

Lifejackets strapped in place
    the wheel tied down
        they huddled close and
            repeated their vows
                of years long past

The gale continued through the
    black, invisible night,
        the unrelenting thundering clatter
            their only companion

Finally, the dawn broke amid
    quieting seas and gentle winds

Their sloop had braved the storm
    and they found themselves
        off the southern shores of Sardinia
            tattered, exhausted but secure

They looked anew at their lives
    and promised to live each
        moment with love and
            appreciation for God's gift
                of new tomorrows

A Desperate Hungry Lover

The sea thrust itself upon us
Like a desperate hungry lover,
Devouring us with its desire,
Throwing us across the cabin
Sole, to crash against the table
Upending chairs, sending charts
And sextant flying from their
Place of hiding.

Dark waters cascading over decks
And bulkheads, relentless and
Unforgiving, angry, demanding
Blinding us with its frothy fury
Determined to wrap its green
Tentacles around us and carry us
Off to its briny lair more than
One hundred fathoms far below
Where it would hold us in rusted
Iron chains, forgotten prisoners,
For centuries to come.

The Despoiler

They built the refinery by the sea
    they should have hidden it away
they cleared and scraped the land
    and laid a scar upon the bay

The brown haze now blacks out the sun
    for most any summer's day
and makes us weep in sorrow
    as whale and dolphin move away.

Where lives the corporate chieftain
    whose wants cut to the bone
Whose greed and indifference to beauty
    are oh so clearly shown?

Why he lives in a pristine palace
    many leagues from here
with not a factory to be found
    with his precious family near.

He scars not the land
    which nourishes his family well
no, only the land where
    my friends and I must dwell.

Isla Espirito Santo

The sun danced gingerly across
the topaz waters of the bay
and then came to rest on the
fishermen's shacks, painting
them with a palette of ochre
and crimson.

The fishermen had come to visit
yesterday, trading a bucket
of the smallish Cabrilla fish
for a few bottles of cerveza and
a couple gallons of water.
They had come to their fishing
shacks two weeks ago and
supplies were low.

This morning we had trekked
among the cacti that decorated
the hilltop and then came down
to the sea. We swam leisurely
to our sloop in the inlet
surrounded by a riot of
frigate birds searching for
sea prey.

We had our fishermen's feast
and sang love songs as the
warm afternoon slowly
melted away and the
chill of the evening ended
our day.

We knew that our time
was running short and
soon we would be called
to our other world, but
the memories of Espirito
Santo would always warm
us through the cold of the
winter that lay ahead.

The Aftermath – La Paz 2003

The winds spared no one. The forecast
seemed to change hour by hour.
Finally, the hurricane's fury fell upon
the land.

The telephone towers were the first
to crash and then the docks fell into
the sea and were thrust upon the
unsuspecting shops along the seashore.

The boats anchored in the harbor
were supposedly safe, but it was
a false promise. They cascaded
one upon another across the beach
littering the roadway for miles.

The trees first lost their leaves,
and then their limbs and their
roots, wrenched from the earth
and flung like matchsticks
against the mountainside.

Houses collapsed and furniture
filled the humid air. Autos,
trucks, carts and horses were fired
into the atmosphere like cannon shot
falling from the sky on the unsuspecting
below.

By early morning it was over and the
survivors began to trickle back, to search
for family and friends among the debris.
The death toll was insignificant (unless it
was your loved one) but the multitude
of lives destroyed would sear the town
for generations to come.

God returned to the cathedral the following day.

Sand Castles

I am an expert
at building
          sand castles
towering edifices
with moats
and great halls,
secret passages
and jousting yards.

My castles rise
          majestically,
daring the sea
to exercise its will,
baring their pride
in the face
of inevitable destruction.

Children gather
to view their splendor,
to smile and laugh
and share their
          happiness,
to build the roads
that villagers must use.

Friends,
      fishermen,
            pretty girls,
all partake
of my seaside feast
and soon
a medieval country
create.

But,
    time
works its madness
on our day
and drives
my countrymen
away.

Too soon,
the sun falls down
and brings the tide
to cover up
        my life
leaving in its path
the misshapen mounds
of today's
        triumphs.

The Death of Venice

The sea steals in to Venice
unobserved, insidiously
reclaiming a lost kingdom
capturing a sixteenth of an
inch of land each month
a miniscule fraction but
never ending

Centuries old palazzi
surrendering to the sea
walkways once trod by
Donatello, Titian, and
Tintoretto disappearing
in the acrid smell of
mustard colored canals

The Palazzo Ducalle
commanding a weary
Piazza San Marco watches
over the decaying city
the glory of a seagoing
empire, the home of
Marco Polo, the bastion
of ancient trade, the source
of silks, papers, teas, and spices

The home of Vivaldi's church
of La Pieta with the sounds
of Le Quatro Staggione
drifting beneath the fading
frescos of Tiepolo, while the
sea laps at its foundation

The generous patron of art
architecture, music and poetry
the womb of seventeenth
century culture, slowly
sinking, losing its place
in the modern world
inch by inch

The Fishermen of Ponza

The fishing boats leave
On the wings of morning
Slipping out of the harbor
Leaving far astern
The shadows of the night

Much has changed in
The small Italian seaport
But the life of the fishermen
Is much the same

Decades have meant little
To the colorful boats that
Still ply the seas in search of
The declining bounty of a
Polluted Mediterranean Sea

The fishermen still live
On the edge of the precipice
Money is always a quest
Sons far too often
Leave family and friends
For the excitement of Rome

The Bishop still blesses the fleet
With a hopeful prayer for
Safety and abundance
The storms still carry away
Their desperate brothers
And widows still weep
In the lookout above the bay

Santa Cruz Island

A journey back in time
Island bathed in silence
Mysterious sounds whispering
Through brambles, listen for
The boar snorting in its lair
Watch the island fox ambling
Down the crusted roadway
With a young one trailing
Gingerly in its wake.

Venerated land of the Chumash
Tribe, two thousand strong
Living peacefully with nature's
Bounty only to be decimated
By a white man's plague, then
Escaping to an uncertain future
On an unwelcoming mainland.

Pioneer families Caire, Gherini,
Christy and Stanton bringing
Sheep and cattle, alfalfa and
Island hay, and hillside vineyards
With their red bricked, tin roof
Winery sending its ambrosia to
Los Angeles and San Francisco.

Place of great beauty, with
Wildflowers spilling over rock
Cliffs and crawling up from
Canyons. Goldfields covering
San Pedro Point, bush poppy,
Snow barrow, silver lotus,
Golden yarrow, yellow monkey
Flower and checker bloom
With its rose blanket of early
Spring hope.

Birds chattering and parading
From mountain peak to valley,
From inlet, to cove, to broad bay,
Brown pelicans, and black
Oyster crackers, and sapphire
Colored jays, long billed curlews,
Whimtrels, and snowy plovers,
Covering the island with a
Chorus of joy.

A place of ancient, timeless beauty,
A window to a forgotten world,
A place of refuge from the tumult
And terror of an anxious new century.

The Seafarer

The beard was white, the hair
In a speckled pony tail, the
Back stooped, the skin pocked,
The eyes clouded.

The pack on his shoulder was
Much heavier than in days
Gone by.

As he walked down the dock
A young girl approached and
Asked to take his picture.
He had become picturesque.

Growing old was a bitch.
No one wanted a seventy
Year old first mate.
Experience be damned, he
Had outlived his usefulness.

All those ships, and ports and
God, how many women,
All jumbled together, one upon
Another in the far recesses of
His mind.

Soon they would disappear,
And he would be left with a
Barren life, away from the
Sea that kept him alive.

He prayed his sister wouldn't
Put him in a box and stick him
In the ground. Hopefully, the
Seamen's Union would honor
His ashes with a burial at sea.

That was all that was left.

Stolen Dreams

My recollection is unsure
    veiled in mystic clouds,
perhaps it was on a
    quiet windswept beach
on a far distant
    magical wondrous isle.
We lay on the sand
    and dreamed sweet dreams.
My dreams were always
    and only of you
and the enchanting lands
    we might yet explore.
But time can be like
    a thief in the night
stealing youthful dreams
    creating opaque memories
leaving only the blowing dust
    of yesterday's reveries.

All Wrong

The wrong country

The wrong port

The wrong bar

The wrong drink

The wrong song

The wrong woman

The wrong dance

The wrong boyfriend

The wrong argument

The wrong fight

The wrong hospital

The Anchor

Forged iron
blackened, hard
massive
ship of the line
king's servant
sailing seven seas
battle ready
duty
unrelenting
victory, glory
battle tough
digging deep
duty
battle weary
holding fast
unrelenting
never giving way
decommissioned
rusting, resting
unmovable mystery

The Sky…

Skies

I love to gaze on clouds.
Their chariots of reflected
sunlight often carry me to
places of hope and renewal.

The Nimbus with their
ominous portents, their
bluster and self-importance,
their painter's palette of gray
and white with at times a
flash of lavender. I love even
the rain and snow they often
fling down.

The wispy Cirrus drifting
high across a sapphire sky,
their chilling ice crystals
carrying a promise of fair
days ahead. They seem to say,
"Do not despair, our father
the sun will warm your days
and brighten your lives."

But most of all, my favorites
are the Cumulus with their
silver towers reaching far up
into the heavens. They call to
me to scale their heights with
a promise of eternal life
if I would only try.

Aloft

Snowy nimbus
Icy cirrus
Towering cumulus

     Silver rivers
     Sapphire lakes
     Emerald bays

       Rugged mountains
       Crouching plains
       Sprawling deserts

Bucolic villages
Monotonous suburbs
Weary cities

Wizened farms
Sprawling ranches
Patterned vineyards

Scarring mines
Smoking factories
Silicon valleys

A Poet's Wandering

Just before dusk
I wandered into
the autumn woods;
a poet's quest
for inspiration.

Would the quiet
bring forth the ghosts
of Lowell and Jeffers
or even my old friend
Carlos Williams?

The path I traveled
came to a fork;
I carried on
thinking of Frost,
then I hesitated.

Did I take
the wrong path
which will make
no difference at all?

I turned and
quickly retreated
from the woods.

lunch at cima linda

a gigantic blue heron
moving south for a
cabo san lucas holiday
stopped by the water
garden at cima linda
for a gourmet lunch
he had heard from
friends that the menu
was simply superb and
a quick look confirmed
their excellent taste
he started with two
golden ogan koi as an
appetizer and then enjoyed
two showa sanke as a
main course followed by
a lovely orange and white
hikai muji for dessert
taking out his travel
guide he made note
to return next year
bowing to me when
he recognized the maitre d'
and with a modest belch
he spread his wings and
flapped a noisy adieu

Lunar Eclipse

The moon sent a love beam
    into my bedroom and it
        tripped across the carpet
           and rested on my cheek.

I was not in the mood
    for love beams, and
        turned my head and
           smothered it with a pillow.

Moments passed and the
    beam was still there
        casting an unwelcome light
           on my tired, exasperated face.

It would not leave me alone,
    its romantic misty light
        nestled on our bed
           beseechingly.

Convinced there was only one solution
    I turned and kissed my lady love.
        The moon smiled
           then slowly left the room
               as a cloud ushered it away.

A Warm Blanket

Your love
    is my warm blanket
on a frosty, frigid
    winter's morn
wrapped around me
    close, tightly,
holding off tomorrow
    protecting me
from the displacency
    of the day to come
promising solace
    at the end
of my chilling hours
    away

Look Back in Laughter

As I look back on a life
of three score and then some
I wonder at how I arrived
at this place.

A trip that has seen me
travel from the inner city
to the pastoral university
village, and then to exciting
urban life.

A trip through the corporate
world and then to a faculty
position, and then once again
back to corporate life, and
finally a peaceful retirement
in a lovely coastal town.

In looking back I see a
sustaining force. What was
it that kept me sane and
sound as I traveled through
an often insane world?

Love of course stands out
as a wonderful, consuming,
comforting factor. To love
and be loved in return is a
special blessing that far too
few enjoy.

But beyond love lies
laughter. The ability to
find humor in the mundane.
The knack of finding wit
among the witless. The
confidence to laugh at
oneself and find humor
in one's personal tragedies.

The ability to celebrate
life with laughter and
joy, and most importantly
to share it with others.

Singing in the Rain

The yellow moon
hangs hidden
                from the lemon tree
while green rain thrashes
down
        down
                down
creating its noisy silence

An honest freshness
covers my face
                with the impotent stings
                of infant bees
swarming over shoulders
plastering cloth on skin
hard across my back

New rivers
                in rivulets
roll over cobblestones
drowning dancing feet
with clutching torrents

Car lights splash
                    across my eyes
                    leaving brown stains
running
        at my knees

Shouting
    laughing
        singing
amid my purification rite

I mark the scene
Gene Kelly
I love you

Overwhelmed

Too many things to do

and places to see

and women to love

and friends to flee

and games to play

and people to be.

Waiting for the Light

Standing on the corner
New York early evening
Waiting for the light
Gentle rain falling
In an autumn caress
You appear in the mist
Across the silver street
Almost forgotten memories
Of a young romance
Warm hungry bodies
Rolling across tired sheets
Making breathless promises
Filled with untruths
A bus sneaks between us
And then moves on
Carrying you away
To today's anxious lover
Leaving behind only
Empty distant illusions

Black Night Journey

I tossed and turned last night,
my body roiling my restless mind.

Too many things undone
wrapped around missing pieces
and endless questions.

Yesterdays filled with mystic
travels to the far reaches of
consciousness searching the
philosopher's cabinet.

Journeys to Tibetan monasteries
and Jesuit retreats challenged by
existentialist passions.

Lying on a Roman terrace with
Cicero and Cato lamenting the
passing of their golden world.

Sailing with Byron and Shelley
on storm-filled Tyrrhenian Seas
searching for scraps of meaning
in a dissolute life.

Awakening in a peaceful Sardegna
Bay, with the gift of another day
to seek answers.

the dawning

you bring the dawn
    to my winter's night

carrying the atrophied
    dreams of tomorrow

from their long
    abandoned place

back to the edge
    of today's reality

taking my tired temerity
    by the hand

and leading it from
    its place of hiding

into the early morning
    light of what

might still yet be

Remembering Home

Long winged birds soar across
a languorous sky and then in
an instant one seems to fall
as though shot and plunges
into the sweltering sea.

We see it emerge with a
struggling fish clamped tight
within its beak and then bank
and skim the water as it hurries
to its distant nest.

We watch and wait in
the evening's early quiet
for the sun to take its
leave. An emerald flash
appears in the far horizon
and we know it is over.

I think of the home I
fled so many months ago
and finally remember why.

the wind song of the gentle flowering wood

the autumn woods
wrapped in their warm coat
of many colors

call out to life's weary traveler
promising peace
and a place of refuge

the woods have always offered
tranquility and succor
to the forgotten and forlorn

even in winter when the leaves
have given up their life
and floated to the earth

and an early frost has laid
a chilling hand
on naked branches

the stillness of the wood
delivers a promise of peace
a message of hope

and we can once again
look forward to spring and rejoice
that god has not abandoned us

and that redemption lives
in the wind song
of the gentle flowering wood

The Attic

The attic seemed always foreboding.
A place of unheard footsteps and
cries in the night. The door at the
top of the stairs was always locked.
I was never sure whether it was
to keep someone out or to lock
in something of great terror.

When I was eleven years old I
became more courageous and asked
my grandmother to take me up
those stairs. She opened a door
to a gray world of battered old
trunks, discarded bureaus, long
abandoned dollhouses and scattered
boxes of trinkets and ancient books.
I spent an entire afternoon entranced
by our hidden family treasures.

In an old wooden box I discovered
my great, great grandmother Winthrop's
family bible. The brown-edged
yellow pages clutching each other
in an attempt to maintain order.

There, I found an obituary for
her cherished son who fought
for the Union and fell at Antietam.
A graduate of Harvard at nineteen
who did not have to fight that war.
A boy of incredible promise who
died like thousands of other boys
sent to war by old men in safe
distant offices.

Teardrops still stained the clipping
from the Boston Globe. One hundred
years and more could not
contain a mother's grief as she
passed eternity in sorrow.

I placed the bible carefully
back in the sacred box and
never visited the attic again.

Approaching Manhood

Watching my son
    approach manhood
        I tremble.
What a perilous journey
    lies before him.
I think of challenges
    I faced
        in a far less
            complex world.
I see him carving
    out his own life and
        separating himself
in not too subtle ways
    from my wisdom.
I find myself now
    regarded as flawed
        and too conventional,
            even weird.

The wisdom of a few years
        past has now disappeared,
                hopefully,
to be born again in the
        not too distant years.
Occasionally,
        when illness strikes,
                my young son returns.
He seeks my comfort.
But then he recovers
        and strides out again
                on his own.
I settle in to wait
        for my wisdom and
                sound judgment to re-emerge,
                        hopefully,
when he becomes a man.

Raspberry Swirl

I worked one summer
for an ice cream man,
two blocks away
from Aunt Pearl's
house on Cherry Street.

My first real job;
I was underage, but
in a small country town
in Pennsylvania
no one really cared.

My mother was a vanilla
and chocolate woman;
no other flavor ever
made its way home
from the supermarket.

But the ice cream man bought
fresh strawberries and peaches
and raspberries and rhubarb
and we made glorious ice cream.

Betty Lou was fourteen,
two years older than I
but she was my first love.
I think she loved me as well
but looking back I believe
she probably loved my
raspberry swirl much more.

The Stationmaster

My favorite uncle was
a stationmaster with the
Pennsylvania Railroad.
A big powerful man with
a bit of a swagger and
a gravelly voice.

When I was nine years
old he took me to the
stationhouse. His office
was bigger than our
living room in Lewistown.

He had a large mahogany
desk with a chair six feet
tall. I looked up to him.
His voice was the voice of
God. The railroad men gave
him their respect. They
called him Sir.

He had a long silver chain
with a gold pocket watch
that never stopped. He made
the trains run on time.

Black fireboxes belching
smoking coal from the
deep, dark, terror-filled mines,
driving soot-covered bullets,
carrying my aunt to New York.

Author, Author

The occasion was a dear friend's
new book, published after an
arid hiatus of some twenty years.
A desert time when words lay
buried in the sand of some
far distant land.

Now, a rebirth with words
flowing once again. They would
arrive in the middle of the night,
in the heat of midday, or early
in an evening's sunset. A torrent
of words falling one upon another
in a cloudburst of thought.

The attention, while well-deserved
puzzled him, the plague of self
doubt still existed in the recesses
and corners of his mind. Was this
creative explosion the end? Was
this naught but a writer's death knell?

I comforted him as best I could, reassuring him that this rebirth was truly a beginning. The phoenix had arisen from the ashes to fly to distant shores, to carry him to places of which he could only dream.

The Rat Catcher's Wife

I found her headstone,
close by the old church
at Chipping Norton village.

Her husband John's work
was that of a wanderer,
village to village,
town to town
always moving on.

A hard, friendless life,
lonely, sad, degrading,
with no place or time
for family.

Wanderings far behind
her now, she still
sleeps in his shadow.

But the hours
flow more softly here
with the gentler spirits
of the deep wood.

Tuscan Morning

The sun awakened
    to a lavender day
and raised a wary eye
    then blinked
        a yellow sky.
The Tuscan roof tiles
    far below
sent their orange reflection
    blazing across
        the cold morning.
The hillside vineyards
    reached out for the
        day's warm caress
as the bells of San Gregorio
    peeled out in
        joyous rapture.
Once again God
    had given his blessing
        to his chosen ones.

The Countess

She was an innocent abroad.
She married the Count at
her mother's urging. It was a
time when desperation had
reduced his haughtiness. He had
abandoned his pedestal next to
the gods and had become
mortal. His creditors had lost
their patience. Their letters
dominated his daily mail.

She arrived with a modest
fortune, which at first had been
appreciated, but soon was the
subject of disdain, as the
gambling debts took their
toll and overwhelmed it.

The palazzo by the lake had been
lost, and they found themselves
living hand-to-mouth in a bizarre
noblesse obligé way. Pretense
had replaced substance. Love
was lost on a cruel man. She lived
under his heavy yoke.

When he made his last wager and lost the palazzo in Rome, she knew he was close to the end. His death was largely unmourned and only a minor footnote to a dreary opera season.

But she had escaped from bondage. Her oppressor was no more. In a strange way, the Count would have understood. Life had dealt her a new hand, and she liked the cards.

About the Author

The over-used descriptive "renaissance man" is certainly appropriate regarding Robert Emmons. Corporate executive, international consultant, university professor, entrepreneur, philanthropist, art collector, and poet all can be genuinely applied to the author of *The Wanderer.*

Emmons has been the recipient of numerous awards from the business community, including the University of Southern California's Marshall School of Business Executive of the Year Award and *International Distributor Magazine*'s Food Industry Hall of Fame Award. He has also received a number of honors for his philanthropy and community-service efforts, including the Herbert Hoover Humanitarian Award, the Santa Barbara Museum of Art's Wright Ludington Lifetime Achievement Award, and the City of Hope's Community Leader Award.

An accomplished author, Emmons has six books to his credit. His first volume of poetry, *Other Places, Other Times,* Literary Arts 1973, was called "a gem of a book" by *Los Angeles Times* critic William Murphy. Pulitzer Prize-winning author and poet N. Scott Momaday, commenting on Emmons after the publication of his volume *The Road to Paradise,* Capra

Press 2003, said, "Robert Emmons…is thought, perception, and imagination personified. He sees beyond the superficial aspects of experience to the realities at the center of our lives. The invitation is to wonder, to delight, to solace, to discovery, to the sacred within us. We accept, and we are enriched in the acceptance."

One thousand hardcover copies of *The Wanderer* were printed by Capra Press in 2004. Twenty-six copies in slipcases have been lettered and signed by the author.

About Capra Press

Capra Press was founded in 1969 by the late Noel Young. Among its authors have been Henry Miller, Ross Macdonald, Margaret Millar, Edward Abbey, Anais Nin, Raymond Carver, Ray Bradbury, and Lawrence Durrell. It is in this tradition that we present the new Capra: literary and mystery fiction, lifestyle and poetry.

Contact us. We welcome your comments.

Capra Press
155 Canon View Road
Santa Barbara, CA 93108
www.caprapress.com

A Note on the Typeface

ITC Berkeley Oldstyle is a Tony Stan redrawing of Frederic Goudy's original Californian typeface, created in 1938 for the University of California Press in Berkeley. It contains much of Goudy's original Californian design and adds features of other Goudy typefaces such as Kennerley, Goudy Oldstyle, Deepdene and Booklet Oldstyle. Characterized by its calligraphic elegance and subtlety, ITC Berkeley Oldstyle is easy to read and pleasurable to the eye.